T

Adapted by Shannon Eric Denton
Illustrated by Mark Pennington

WAYLAND

First published in 2014 by Wayland

Copyright © 2014 Wayland

Wayland
338 Euston Road
London NW1 3BH

Wayland Australia
Level 17/207 Kent Street
Sydney, NSW 2000

Adapted Text by Shannon Eric Denton
Illustrations by Mark Pennington
Colours by Robby Bevard
Edited by Stephanie Hedlund
Interior Layout by Kristen Fitzner Denton and Alyssa Peacock
Book Design and Packaging by Shannon Eric Denton
Cover Design by Alyssa Peacock

Copyright © 2008 by Abdo Consulting Group

A cataloguing record for this title is available at the British Library.
Dewey number: 398.2'452-dc23

Printed in China

ISBN: 978 0 7502 7834 8

Wayland is a division of Hachette Children's Books, an Hachette UK company.
www.hachette.co.uk

One sunny day, a hare sat by a tree.

The hare watched a tortoise approach.

The tortoise was slow.

The hare laughed at the slow tortoise.

'You're the slowest thing I've ever seen!' the hare said.

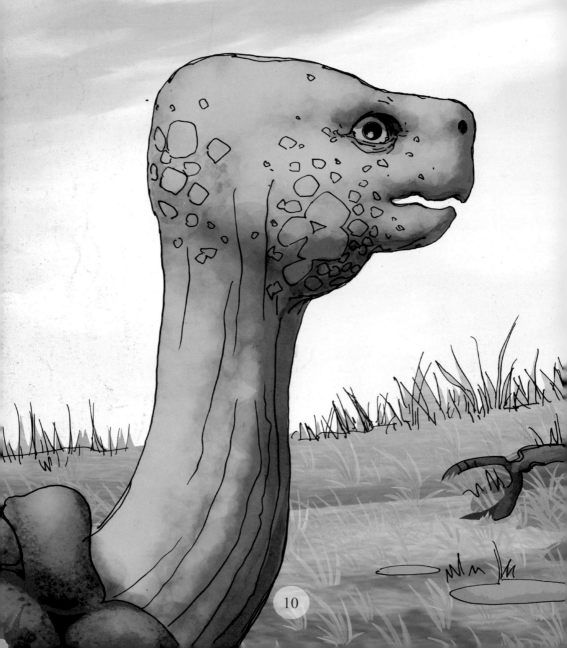

'You shouldn't make fun of me' said the tortoise.

'There is nothing you can do about it' the hare said.

14

'That's not true' said the tortoise.

'Do you want to race?' asked the tortoise.
The hare couldn't stop laughing.

The hare agreed, and soon they were racing.

The hare ran very far ahead of the tortoise.

22

23

'You'll never catch me' laughed the hare.

The hare grew tired and decided to take a nap.

While the hare slept, the tortoise slowly continued.

FINI

The moral of the story is:

Slow and steady wins the race!